ANIMAL CELLS
AND LIFE PROCESSES

Barbara A. Somervill

HEINEMANN LIBRARY

Chicago, Illinois

www.capstonepub.com
Visit our website to find out
more information about
Heinemann-Raintree books.

To order:
☎ Phone 800-747-4992
🖥 Visit www.capstonepub.com
to browse our catalog and order online.

Edited by Megan Cotugno and Andrew Farrow
Designed by Philippa Jenkins
Original illustrations © Capstone Global Library, Ltd.
Illustrated by KJA-artists.com
Picture research by Hannah Taylor
Production by Alison Parsons
Originated by Capstone Global Library, Ltd.

Library of Congress Cataloging-in-Publication Data
Somervill, Barbara A.
  Animal cells and life processes / Barbara A.
Somervill.
      p. cm. -- (Investigating cells)
  Includes bibliographical references and index.
  ISBN 978-1-4329-3877-2 (hc)
  1. Cells--Juvenile literature. 2. Life (Biology)--
Juvenile literature. I. Title.
  QH582.5.S66 2011
  571.6′1--dc22
                            2009049971

Acknowledgments
The author and publishers are grateful to the
following for permission to reproduce copyright
material: Agefotostock: J & C Sohns, 13, Reinhard
Dirscherl, 31 top, Rodolfo Benítez, 4; Alamy:
BIOSPHOTO, 36, Frans Lemmens, 41, INTERFOTO,
11, Somos Images, 43, The Africa Image Library,
30, Tim Hill, 21; Capstone Studio: Karon Dubke,
16, KJA-artists.com, 8, 9, 10, 12, 23, 25, 33, 34,
39; Getty Images: Maximilian Stock Ltd., 22,
UniversalImagesGroup, 5, Victoria Stone & Mark
Deeble, 18, Werner Bollmann, 14; iStockphoto:
benjaminalbiach, 37, levkr, 40, Ikordela, 7; Science
Source: A. Syred, 29, Astrid & Hanns-Frieder Michler,
24, Bjorn Svensson, 35, CNRI, 42, Dr Gopal Murti, 38,
Equinox Graphics, 31 bottom, Sercomi, cover, Steve
Gschmeissner, 32; Shutterstock: Anke van Wyk, 17,
ESB Professional, 28, Lebendkulturen.de, 27, Merrill
Dyck, 26, neijia, 19, photowind, 6

We would like to thank Michelle Raabe, Ph.D., for
her invaluable help in the preparation of this book.

Every effort has been made to contact copyright
holders of any material reproduced in this book. Any
omissions will be rectified in subsequent printings if
notice is given to the publisher.

Contents

Some words are printed in bold, **like this**. You can find out what they mean by looking in the glossary.

What Is a Cell?

You cut your finger, and a single drop of blood falls. You have just lost millions of cells. Cells are the basic units of all living things. From a blue whale down to a one-celled **protozoa**, animals are made up of individual, microscopic cells.

Everything comes down to the basic unit of life: the cell. Like all other living things, we are nothing more than a bunch of cells. It is how those cells are arranged and what those cells do that makes the difference between different plants and animals.

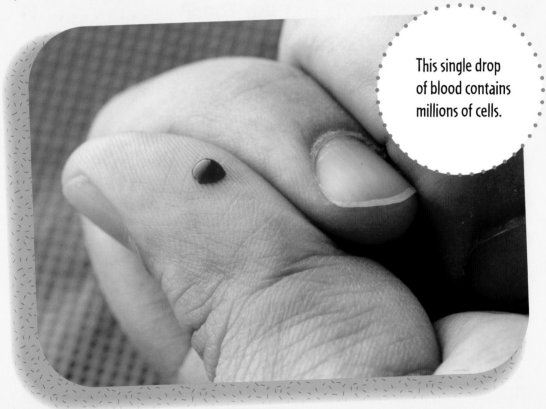

This single drop of blood contains millions of cells.

What do cells do?

In every animal, old cells die and new cells form. Animal bodies are constantly at work. They replace worn-out cells. They make new cells. And every cell has a specific job. Cell work is responsible for all the life processes that keep animals alive and healthy.

How many cells?

As animals grow, the number of cells in their bodies increases. The total number of cells in an animal is tremendous—more than anyone could count. Scientists estimate that adult humans have between 50 trillion and 100 trillion cells. A trillion is a million million! An adult has many more cells than a small child.

Scientist Spotlight
Robert Hooke

Robert Hooke (1635–1703) was one of England's greatest scientists. His natural curiosity led him to study everything from plants to rocks to stars to geology. He even studied the workings of mechanical toys and ships.

His best-known contribution may have been his book *Micrographia* (1665). In this book, Hooke drew accurate illustrations of organisms, or living things, that he saw through a microscope. Hooke described his view of thin slices of cork in *Micrographia*: "The pores of it were not regular . . . these pores, or cells . . . were indeed the first microscopical pores I ever saw." Hooke had discovered plant cells, and we have called these units "cells" since then.

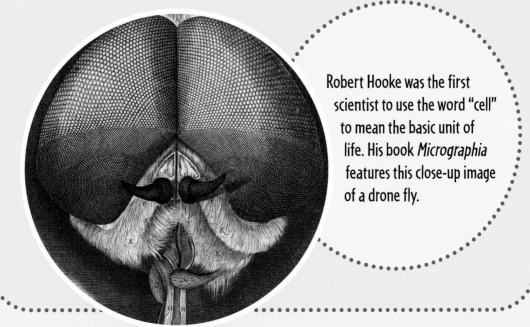

Robert Hooke was the first scientist to use the word "cell" to mean the basic unit of life. His book *Micrographia* features this close-up image of a drone fly.

What basic concepts explain cells?

Scientists who study cells know three truths about animals and plants. These facts make up a theory, or idea, about cells:

1. Every living thing is made up of one or more cells.

2. The cell is the smallest unit of life.

3. All life can be traced to the growth and division of cells.

It is difficult to think that you have much in common with a dandelion or a pine tree, but you do. Looking at human and plant cells show us that we are not that different from plants. We have skin cells that form an outer layer around our bodies. Plants also have cells that form protective skin. Human and plant cells use food for energy, and they also produce waste. In order to grow, our cells **reproduce** (make a copy). To carry on a **species** (group of living things of the same type), plants and animals create offspring.

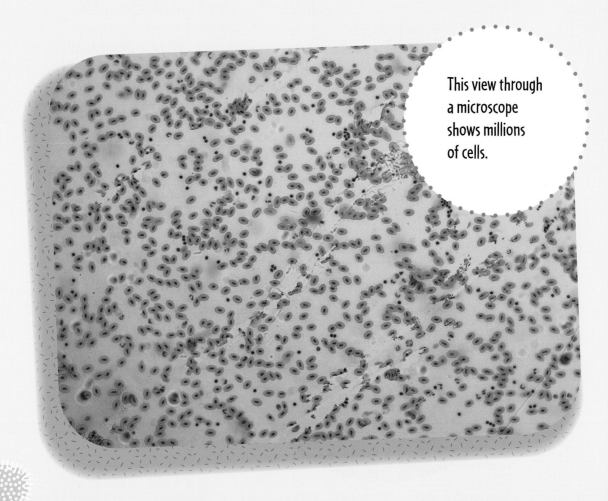

This view through a microscope shows millions of cells.

Science tools: the compound microscope

In 1590 Dutch eyeglass maker Hans Jansen and his son Zacharias put together two magnifying lenses in a tube. They made the first **compound microscope**.

This simple tool opened up the microscopic world to science. Today's microscopes work like the Jansens' microscope, but are much more powerful. They have an upper lens (at the eyepiece) and lenses below. The total magnification equals the power of the eyepiece lens (10x) multiplied by the power of the lower lens (which can be, for example, 4x, 10x, 40x, or 100x). For example, using the 100x lower lens and the 10x eyepiece would magnify an object 1,000 times. This kind of power lets scientists see inside individual cells.

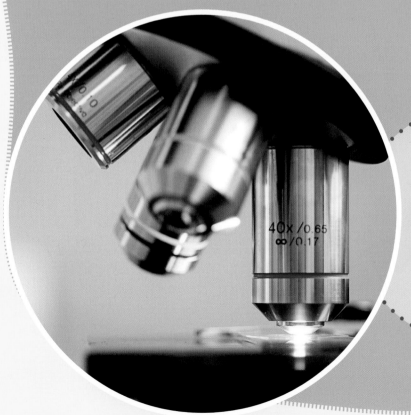

40x /0.65
∞ /0.17

Today's microscopes are powerful enough to see not just cells, but also the parts of cells.

What Are the Parts of an Animal Cell?

Cells, as small as they are, have many parts. Animal cells are eukaryotic cells, which means they have rooms, or chambers, called **organelles**. It helps to think of organelles in terms of the organs in the human body. For example, a human being has a heart, lungs, liver, and kidneys. Each of those organs does a job to keep the body healthy. Animal cell organelles are like microscopic versions of organs. Like the organs in the human body, they each have jobs to do to keep a cell healthy.

Animal cells work 24 hours a day, 7 days a week. They work when you are running or sitting, eating or sleeping. The work cells do happens in organelles. Let's take a closer look at the different parts of an animal cell and what jobs they do.

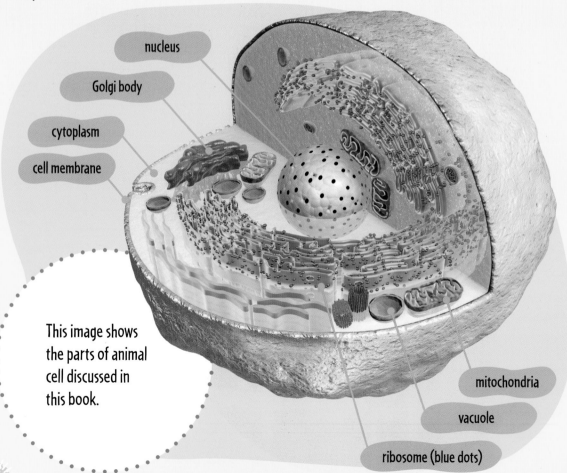

nucleus

Golgi body

cytoplasm

cell membrane

This image shows the parts of animal cell discussed in this book.

mitochondria

vacuole

ribosome (blue dots)

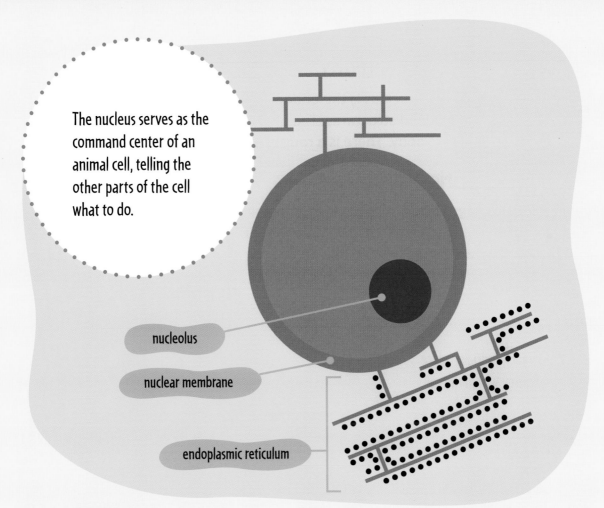

The nucleus serves as the command center of an animal cell, telling the other parts of the cell what to do.

nucleolus

nuclear membrane

endoplasmic reticulum

Membrane

Surrounding an animal cell is the outside "skin" of a cell, called the plasma **membrane** or cell membrane. This membrane is made of **fats**. The plasma membrane is a wall of defense and only lets in what the cell needs to live, like water and food. Inserted in the membrane are various **proteins**.

Inside the nucleus

The **nucleus** is the control center of a cell, like a brain. Like most organelles, it is surrounded by a membrane. It carries directions for such characteristics as height, eye color, and other genetic information (see pages 36–39).

Inside the nucleus is a thread-like structure called chromatin. This is made up of **deoxyribonucleic acid (DNA)** fibers. It is the DNA that provides a map of your body. It decides if you are going to be tall or short, blue or brown eyed, and every other physical thing about you.

Endoplasmic reticulum

Sticking out from the nucleus is the **endoplasmic reticulum (ER)**. This is a network of tube-shaped structures. The ER produces fats and some types of proteins used in the body. There is a rough kind of ER and a smooth kind of ER.

Mitochondria

You need energy to power your body. Your cells also need energy to power their work. A cell's power center is in its **mitochondria**. These organelles have their own DNA. They produce energy to support the cell's main functions.

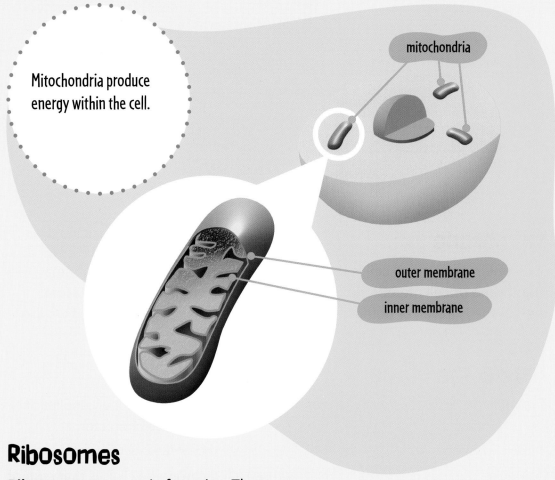

Mitochondria produce energy within the cell.

mitochondria

outer membrane

inner membrane

Ribosomes

Ribosomes are protein factories. These organelles work to turn **ribonucleic acid (RNA)** into proteins. The ribosomes string together **amino acids**. Once a string is complete, it is called a protein.

Golgi body

The **Golgi body** works somewhat like a packaging unit and warehouse. Proteins and **carbohydrates** (sugars and starches) enter the Golgi body. They are covered in thin membranes and sorted into packages. The Golgi body "addresses" each package by putting a chemical message in the membrane that tells where the protein or carbohydrate should be sent.

Scientist Spotlight

Camillo Golgi

Born in Corteno, Italy, Camillo Golgi (1843–1926) was a doctor and scientist with an interest in the workings of cells. Today, we know Golgi as the man who identified the Golgi body in cells.

However, Golgi's greatest work was on the nervous system, for which he won a Nobel Prize in 1906. You might find it strange that Golgi, who ran hospitals and worked in medical labs, never actually practiced as a doctor.

Camillo Golgi dedicated his life to cell research.

Lysosomes

Your stomach helps your body take in **nutrients**. Nutrients are substances that help your body grow and stay healthy. **Lysosomes** are organelles that are like human stomachs. Among other functions, they digest the nutrients that are delivered to a cell. Lysosomes contain chemical substances called **enzymes**, which work like the digestive juices in your stomach.

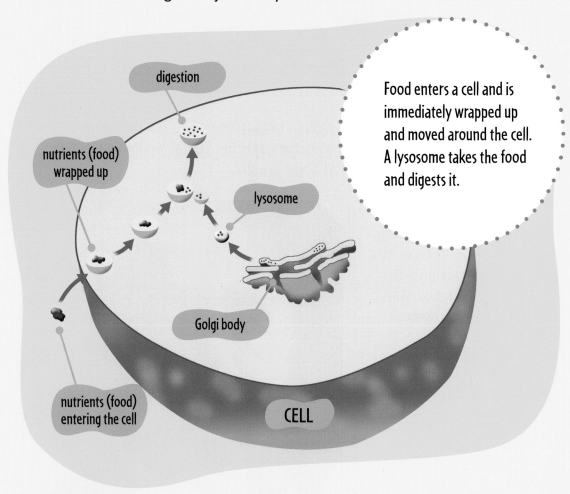

digestion

nutrients (food) wrapped up

lysosome

Golgi body

nutrients (food) entering the cell

CELL

Food enters a cell and is immediately wrapped up and moved around the cell. A lysosome takes the food and digests it.

Cytoplasm

Although cells are extremely tiny, there is still empty space within the cell. **Cytoplasm** is a jellylike substance that fills the space between the nucleus and the cell membrane. It works much like the way egg white fills the space between the yolk and the eggshell in an egg. Organelles float in the cytoplasm.

Vacuoles

Vacuoles also float in cytoplasm. They are pockets containing mostly water that store cell food. When a cell produces protein or food, it stores it in a vacuole, just like you would store a sandwich in a plastic bag.

Organelles also put trash in vacuoles. Cell trash includes broken parts, poisons, and even extra water the cell does not need. To "take out the trash," the vacuole moves to the cell membrane and pushes. The membrane opens, the vacuole opens, and the garbage spills out of the cell. The membrane and the vacuole seal themselves up again and get back to work.

How are organelles and body organs alike?

Animal cells are like the animals they form. They eat, use the energy from food, and take in water. The organelles work like body organs. In some ways, they are more efficient and better organized than humans. When cells are done with something, they immediately get rid of the waste they make.

The cells in this kangaroo have the same organelles that your cells do.

How Do Cells Take In and Use Food?

You eat a ham and cheese sandwich. A giraffe eats leaves. A vulture eats rotting meat from a dead animal. A dung beetle eats . . . you get the idea. Animals take in food to survive.

Despite their size and weight, giraffes get the **nutrients** they need by eating tiny leaves and twigs.

Some animals, like humans, must eat every day. We cannot store enough energy in our bodies to go very long without food. Female whales, on the other hand, go months without feeding, while hummingbirds feed five to eight times an hour.

Animals process foods in different ways and eat different kinds of foods. Herbivores, such as cows and rabbits, eat only plants. Carnivores, such as wolves and lions, eat only meat. Omnivores, such as humans and bears, eat all forms of food.

How much food do animals need to feed their cells?

ANIMAL	WHAT IT EATS	HOW MUCH IT EATS
Cow	Plants (grass, clover)	About 40 kg (88 lbs) a day
Giraffe	Twigs and leaves of trees	About 63 kg (140 lbs) a day
Lion	Meat (usually antelope, zebra, wildebeest)	When hunting is good: Males: 43 kg (95 lbs); Females: 25 kg (55 lbs); Averages out to 8-9 kg (18-20 lbs) a day
Hippo	Plants (grasses, reeds)	40 kg (88 lbs) a night
Gray whale	Mostly small **crustaceans**	330 kg (728 lbs) a day for four months, then nothing for the rest of the year
Dolphin	Fish	About 20 kg (44 lbs) a day
Hummingbird	Nectar	As much as three times their own weight per day
Gray wolf	Meat (from mice to moose)	About 4.5 kg (10 lbs) a day, but they do not always eat daily

What happens to the food we eat?

Let's follow that ham and cheese sandwich from the plate to your cells. You take a bite of sandwich. Cells in your mouth sense the food and produce extra **saliva**, the watery liquid in your mouth. Your chewing and the **enzymes** in the saliva help break down the bread, ham, and cheese. You swallow, sending a mushy pulp into your stomach.

Acid in your stomach breaks down the food into **molecules** (the smallest unit of a substance). A ham and cheese sandwich contains vitamins, minerals, **fats**, **proteins**, sugars, water, and fiber. As the sandwich passes through your intestines, nutrient molecules are absorbed into your body.

Your cells need you to eat a balance of different foods to provide the nutrients they need.

Cells in a lion's body process meat to get protein, fats, sugars, and nutrients they need to work properly.

How do cells use nutrients?

At this point, the cells take over. They use calcium to make strong bone and tooth cells. Iron goes into **red blood cells**. Proteins are used to build muscle cells and support the growth of new cells. The **carbohydrates** in bread are turned into energy to power cells. The fats in the ham and cheese are processed and absorbed into cells. The unused parts of food become waste and pass from the body as **feces**, or solid waste.

No one type of food has all the nutrients human cells need. That is why humans need to eat so many different foods. Cows get all the nutrients their cells need by eating grass. Wolves and lions only eat meat, but their cells process those foods to get all their nutrients from meats. Being a plant eater or meat eater is not a decision animals make. That decision, like nearly everything else, is determined within their cells.

What Products Do Animal Cells Make?

All cells have specific jobs. There are bone cells, blood cells, organ cells, and so on. Cells produce products that help them work properly. Animal cells use four main **molecules**: **proteins**, **nucleic acids**, **carbohydrates**, and **fats**. These molecules produce the materials that make up and run an animal's body.

How do we make and use proteins?

Proteins are found in nearly every living cell and fluid in your body. When you digest proteins, cells break protein down into **amino acids**. The amino acids form chains, and the chains make new proteins. Proteins that you eat are turned into different, more useful proteins in the body.

Your muscles, heart, lungs, stomach, and most **hormones** contain protein. Hormones are chemical substances that control how cells react. Proteins also work in **red blood cells**, helping the cells carry oxygen. Antibodies in your body that fight disease are also proteins.

All animals use proteins, but not always the same way. Keratin, a variety of protein, makes fingernails, tortoise shells, eagle feathers, porcupine quills, and the outer layer of roundworms. On the surface, a feather does not look like a fingernail. But through a microscope, the basic cells of these items look pretty much the same.

This porcupine's quills are made from proteins.

DNA in water buffalo cells determines the size and shape of the animal's horns.

Nucleic acids

There are two basic types of nucleic acid: **RNA** and **DNA**. RNA refers to ribonucleic acid. DNA refers to deoxyribonucleic acid.

Nucleic acids provide the directions that tell cells where to go and what to do. A bone cell, for example, is only a bone cell because DNA told it to be. DNA carries all the information your body needs to determine which types of cells are formed and what those cells do. It is a huge information warehouse. No cell could read through all that information every time it needed to do some work.

Within DNA there are sections called **genes** that code for specific proteins. To make a protein, the DNA code is first copied into a piece of messenger RNA (mRNA). The mRNA leaves the **nucleus** and travels to a **ribosome**, where the gene's code is used to produce a protein.

Where do cells get the energy they need to do work?

Carbohydrates are fuel for animals. They provide the energy cells need to do their work. Carbohydrates should make up 45 to 60 percent of the total calories a person eats each day. There are two types of carbohydrates: simple carbohydrates and complex carbohydrates.

Simple carbohydrates

Animals sometimes need sudden bursts of energy. For example, an animal needs to run from a predator. A burst of energy powers muscle cells to give the fleeing animal speed. That energy comes from simple carbohydrates, or simple sugars.

Simple sugars (such as soda, candy, and jelly) provide fast energy because they are quickly digested. The sugars in these foods are absorbed into the blood quickly. Simple sugars give cells a boost of energy. Although some are stored, most are used up too quickly to be useful over a long period.

Complex carbohydrates

Animal cells also need energy to do normal work, such as digesting food or building new cells. The energy to do that work usually comes from complex carbohydrates, or stored energy.

Complex carbohydrates are often starches like rice, pasta, bread, potatoes, fruits, and vegetables. Your body has to work to change the starch in whole wheat bread into sugar for energy. It takes longer for cells to absorb the bread's energy.

Complex carbohydrates give cells more than just energy. Complex carbohydrates also have other **nutrients** that bodies need. Broccoli and tomatoes have vitamin A. Whole wheat bread and brown rice have protein and B vitamins. Potatoes have vitamin C and iron.

Whole wheat bread is a complex carbohydrate that is a good source of energy.

Do our cells really need fats?

Animals also need fats, which include waxes. Fats are dissolved in the body, processed, and used in cells. The cell **membrane** of animal cells is made up in part of fats. These fats allow water and nutrients into the cell and keep waste products out of the cell. Fats also store energy and help cells use vitamins.

Storing fat

Many animals store fats in their bodies during peak feeding seasons. This helps them survive when food is scarce. Without fats, bears would not be able to sleep through the winter. Whales could not leave Arctic waters to bear their young.

For whales, that fat is blubber, which **insulates** (covers) their bodies from the cold. Blubber also stores carbohydrates, which feed female whales' bodies for months when they head south to give birth to calves. A gray whale cow, for example, will not eat from the time she leaves the Arctic in late winter until she returns the following fall.

The body gets "good fats" from olives, avocados, nuts, and vegetable oils.

Good and bad fats

Animal bodies have fats that are sometimes called "good" or "bad." "Good fats" help animal bodies work better. For humans, good fats come from fish, soybeans, avocados, olives, and nuts. "Bad fats," like fats from beef or pork, are hard for cells to use. They may clog the free flow of blood through the body.

Filled with water

Water is a necessary part of all cells. In fact, nearly two-thirds of your body is made up of water. The **atoms** in water—hydrogen and oxygen—combine with carbon and other **elements** to form the products your body uses to stay healthy. Most animal bodies have anywhere from two-fifths to four-fifths of their mass as water.

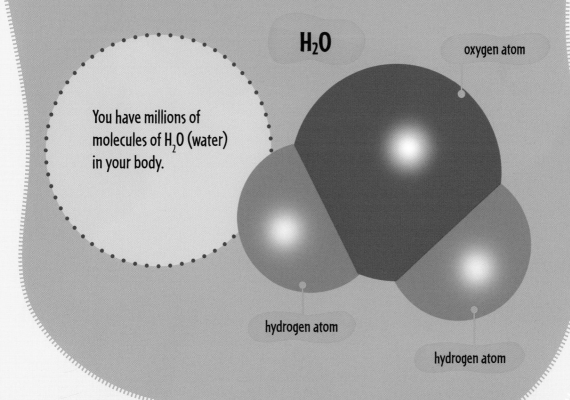

H_2O

oxygen atom

You have millions of molecules of H_2O (water) in your body.

hydrogen atom

hydrogen atom

Can an Animal Really Have Only One Cell?

Some organisms have only one cell. Single-celled organisms (also called unicellular organisms) are not that different from an elephant. They carry on the same life processes that elephants do. They need food and energy. They reproduce so that their **species** will continue. A single-celled organism contains water. It takes in oxygen and rids its body of waste. Elephants function in the same way.

Many single-celled organisms can be seen only through a microscope. These include **amoebas**, **euglenas**, and **paramecia**.

Amoebas

Amoebas are found in ponds and rivers and on the surface of leaves in standing water. They may also live in tropical seas, moist soil, and in larger animals. Amoebas can vary in size, but many measure about 500 to 1,000 **microns** across. One micron is one-millionth of a meter!

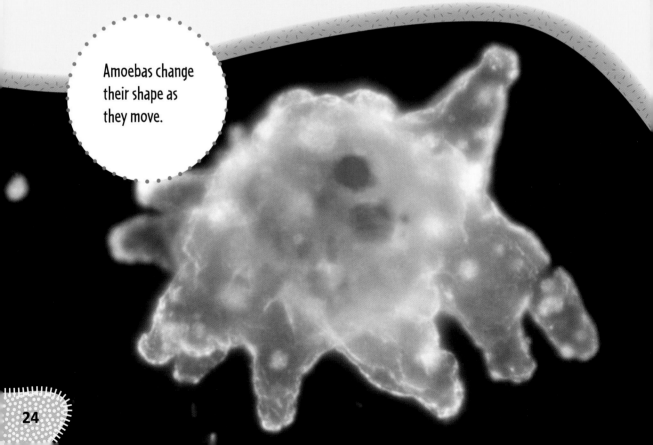

Amoebas change their shape as they move.

Amoebas are jellylike and filled with **cytoplasm**. The word *amoeba* means "change," and that is just what they do. They change shape to move. To eat they change shape and surround the food. They eat **bacteria** (single-celled organisms), **algae** (plantlike organisms that live in water), and animal and plant cells.

Amoebas reproduce by splitting in half, a process called **fission**. When an amoeba produces a new amoeba, the **nucleus** and the cell itself divide in two. The new amoeba is an exact copy of the original one.

What's in the water?

What is living in your local pond? Take a look! With the help of an adult, use a long-handled ladle or a pail to get a small water sample. Put the sample in a white or glass dish. Look through a microscope. You will find several **protists**. Freshwater ponds provide the ideal conditions for small creatures to survive. There is water, food, and warmth from the Sun near the surface. Remember never go to a pond without an adult, and always wash your hands after touching pond water.

A microscope reveals the creatures that live in pond water. Yuck!

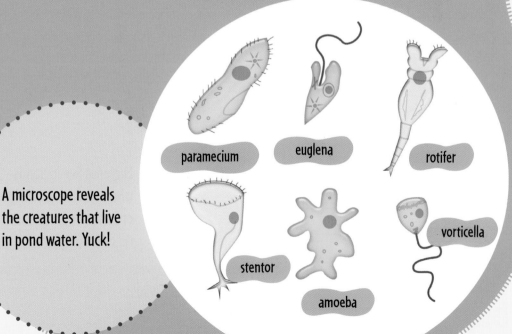

paramecium

euglena

rotifer

stentor

amoeba

vorticella

Euglenas

Euglenas are like plants and animals combined. Like a plant, they have a **chemical compound** (substance made up of two or more **elements**) called chlorophyll. When in sunlight, euglenas, like green plants, use chlorophyll to make energy. In the darkness, euglenas get their own food and energy by eating small plants and animals, as animals do. Euglenas have small, whipping tails that allow them to move in water.

Euglenas are even smaller than amoebas. They measure 25 to 100 microns. They have tiny red eyespots in their cells. These spots react to light. They help euglenas move toward sunlight when they are in a green, scummy pond.

Euglenas live in ponds where they feed on algae or on other protists if there is no light.

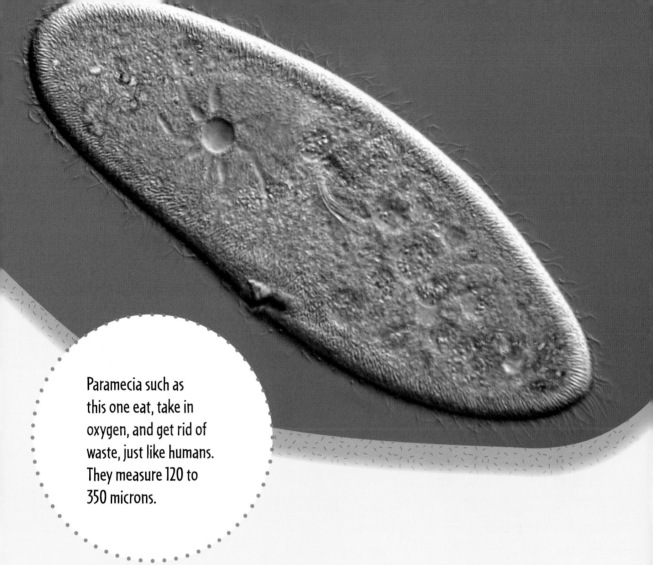

Paramecia such as this one eat, take in oxygen, and get rid of waste, just like humans. They measure 120 to 350 microns.

Paramecia

Paramecia live in ponds with green algae because that is their main food source. They are slipper-shaped animals with tiny hairs all around their cell **membrane**. The hairs, called cilia, allow them to move much like centipedes with their many legs.

Paramecia reproduce through fission, just like amoebas. A paramecium has two nuclei, one large and one small. When it **reproduces**, the smaller nucleus splits in half. One half travels to the far end of the paramecium. Then the larger nucleus splits, and half moves to join the first, smaller split nucleus. The new large and small nuclei remain together as the cell splits, and a new paramecium is formed.

How Are We Different From Amoebas?

The simplest explanation for what makes humans different from **amoebas** is our cells. Human bodies contain 210 different types of cells. Amoebas have only one cell. Our bodies use different cells to form blood, bones, organs, muscles, and so on. The cells that make up a heart are different from cells in the brain or lungs. For amoebas, there is only one cell to carry out all the functions of blood, bones, organs, and muscles.

Yet amoebas, despite their size, carry out all the same life processes that your body does. They take in oxygen, use **nutrients** for cell functions, and eliminate waste. They move by changing their shape. Amoebas may not grow much in size, but they mature and eventually **reproduce**. They are sensitive to light, heat, and cold. The life processes that define a human body are present in even the smallest of animals.

Humans have 210 different types of cells, which form all the organs and other parts of the body.

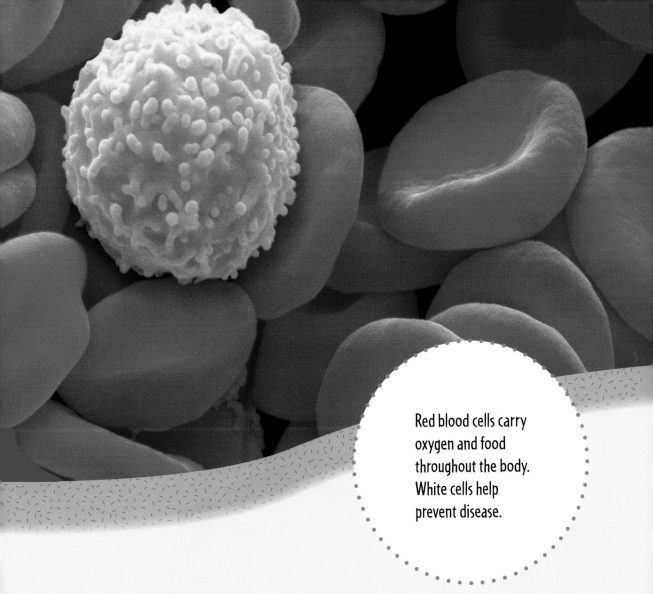

Red blood cells carry oxygen and food throughout the body. White cells help prevent disease.

What cells make up blood?

Blood travels through the entire body. A closer look shows that blood contains **red blood cells**, **white blood cells**, and **platelets**.

Red blood cells are transportation units. They carry oxygen to tissues, bones, and organs, and they take carbon dioxide away. Red blood cells need iron and copper to be healthy. White blood cells are warriors that fight **infection** (illness) and disease.

Platelets are not cells, but are cell fragments that are like cellular glue. They bind wounds together to protect you when you are cut. When skin is cut and blood begins to seep out of a body, platelets rush to the site. Phosphorus and vitamin K help platelets make blood clots.

How do skin, nail, and hair cells work?

Human bodies constantly produce new skin, hair, and nail cells. Skin cells form the body's largest organ. Skin cells form three main layers of skin: the epidermis (top layer), the dermis (middle layer), and the hypodermis (lowest layer), which is made of fat and connective tissue.

In the dermis layer, new skin cells are born. These new cells push the older cells above them into the epidermis. As skin cells are pushed farther up and away from blood vessels, they die out and fall off. Skin cells help regulate body temperatures. They store water and make vitamin D and protect us from heat, injury, and infection. Hair, fingernail, and toenail cells also work to keep our body temperature even and protect us from injuries.

Skin and hair cells also carry pigment, or color. Your skin and hair color come from this pigment in your cells. All animals have pigment in their skin, fur, feathers, or scales. Pigment lets a chameleon's skin color change and makes a grasshopper blend in with the grass.

Skin cells can do some amazing things. This chameleon has cells that allow it to change color!

Why do some animals glow in the dark?

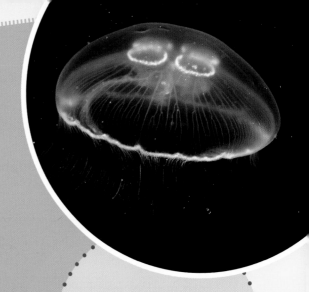

Some animals, such as moon jellies and krill, can glow in the dark. This process is called bioluminescence. This process occurs when certain chemicals bind together with oxygen. When threatened, krill huddle together and glow, swirling around and confusing their enemies. Moon jellyfish glow to attract and signal mates.

These moon jellyfish glow because of a chemical called luciferin in their cells.

What are neurons?

Animals can feel, taste, smell, touch, hear, and see because of nerve cells. Nerve cells, called **neurons**, send messages to the brain. For example, when you touch something hot, your nerve cells sense the heat. They send an instant warning to the brain, and the brain sends a message back to pull away from the heat.

Neurons deal with senses and relay messages from the brain for your heart to beat, your muscles to flex, and your eyes to blink. Humans have large brains. Their brains contain about 100 billion neurons.

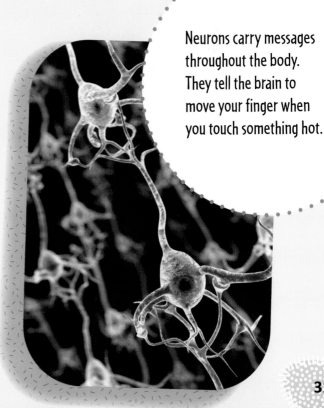

Neurons carry messages throughout the body. They tell the brain to move your finger when you touch something hot.

Are all bone cells the same?

Animals with bones have three types of bone cells. Osteoblast cells form new bone. They do this by **secreting** bone material around themselves until they are trapped. The trapped cells are still alive but are now called osteocytes. Osteoclast cells dissolve old or damaged bone to make room for new bone construction.

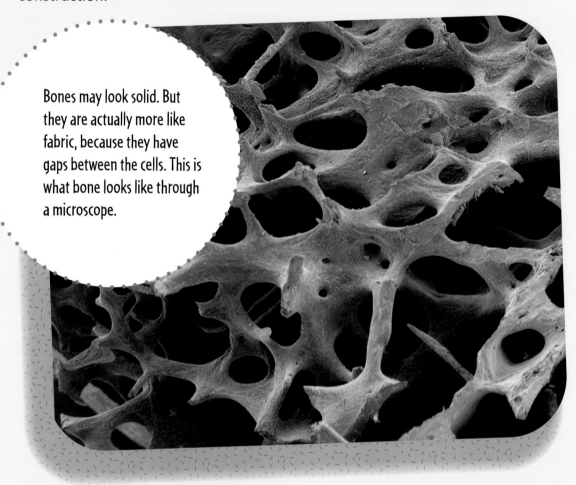

Bones may look solid. But they are actually more like fabric, because they have gaps between the cells. This is what bone looks like through a microscope.

What chemicals are in our bodies?

Humans and other animals need chemicals in our bodies to digest food, use nutrients, and do many other jobs. These chemicals may be **hormones**, **enzymes**, or acids, which are produced by gland cells. These glands release chemicals into the body. They determine how we grow, mature physically, and what kind of mood we are in.

What cells protect us inside the body?

Skin on the outside of our bodies protects us from harm. Inside the body, we have cells that line many of our organs. They do the same job as skin. These cells line the mouth, throat, stomach, lungs, intestines, and colon. They act like walls. They control how water and other substances move in and out of the body. They prevent the **bacteria** living in our intestines from attacking the rest of our body.

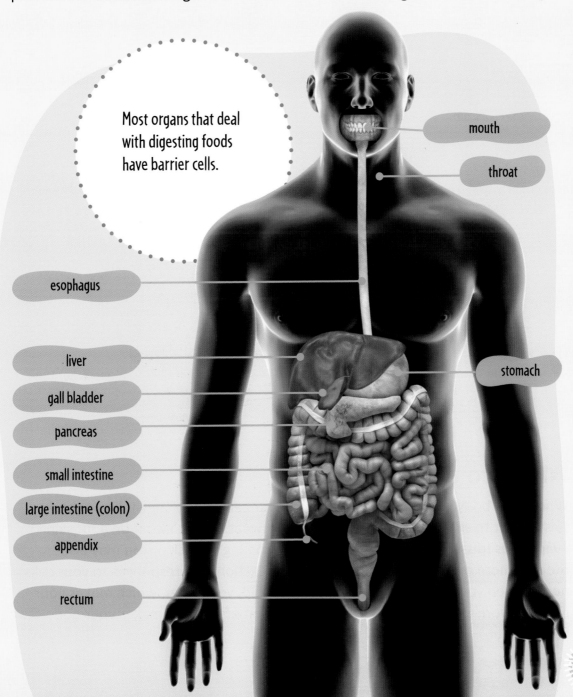

Most organs that deal with digesting foods have barrier cells.

mouth

throat

esophagus

liver

gall bladder

pancreas

small intestine

large intestine (colon)

appendix

rectum

stomach

What Messages Do Cells Send in an Animal's Body?

Did you know that your cells are busily sending messages throughout your body? They are. Cells continually organize our life processes.

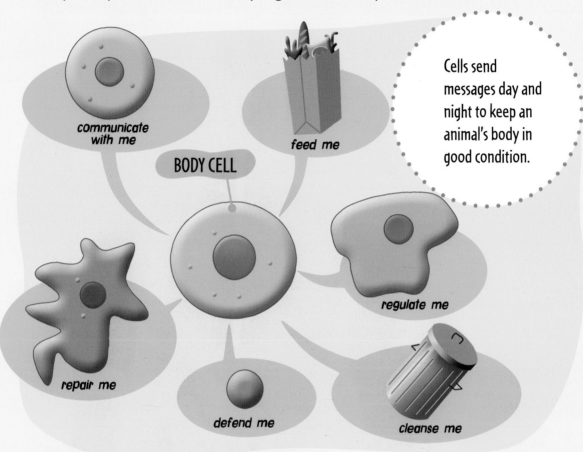

communicate with me

feed me

BODY CELL

regulate me

repair me

defend me

cleanse me

Cells send messages day and night to keep an animal's body in good condition.

What are cell reactions?

When your body gets too hot or too cold, your cells react. They tell your body to sweat or to shiver. If you are too hot, you sweat. As the sweat on your skin evaporates (dissolves), it carries away heat, cooling your skin. You may also breathe more or drink something cold. These actions are responses to your cells' needs when your body is too hot. If you are cold, you shiver, which makes your muscles work and blood rush into the skin. A bit of exercise makes your body feel warmer.

Why do cells need defense?

Cells constantly come under attack from viruses, **bacteria**, and other invaders. When this happens, cells send a message. Other cells come to the rescue, attacking the invader.

Cells also get damaged from daily use and may need repair. Some cells can repair themselves. Other parts are thrown out as garbage. If this happens, the discarded cell is replaced with a new cell. Cells send messages that cause new cells to be produced.

If you are cut badly and lose blood, your cells work overtime. Bone marrow gets the message and makes more **red blood cells** and **white blood cells**. If an **infection** happens, bone marrow increases white blood cell production. Animal bodies constantly build, rebuild, and replace cells.

Cell messages

Messages sent from cells give orders for when to make more of whichever types of cells are needed. When you have enough blood, skin, or bone cells, for example, cells send messages to stop producing new cells. They also know when it is time to take out the trash to get rid of dead cells.

When dogs get overheated, they pant. Panting brings cooler air into the body and lowers the temperature of cells.

If Cells Do Not Grow, How Do Animals Get Bigger?

Ostrich eggs lay in a nest. Within those eggs, new life is growing. The cells that make up the egg divide and form new cells at a fantastic rate. They divide, divide, and divide—again and again. Six weeks later, scraggly ostrich chicks break through their eggshells. Over a year later, the chicks will be full sized. This growth occurs because of cell division.

These hatching ostrich chicks grow at a very fast rate.

What do genes do?

You cannot build a house without a plan. An ostrich chick cannot grow to full size without a plan, either. That plan is written down on the **DNA** in each bird's cells. All living things have DNA. It serves as a blueprint for every characteristic of a worm, an ostrich, and you. Your DNA is unique to you. Even if you are an identical twin, your DNA is not exactly like that of your twin.

DNA contains **genes**, which are individual directions. There are genes for skin color and hair color, the size and shape of your teeth, and the size and shape of your toes. Every cell in your body contains 25,000 to 35,000 genes. The genes line up in strings called **chromosomes**, which work in pairs. You get half of your genes from your mother and the other half from your father. That is why you look like your parents.

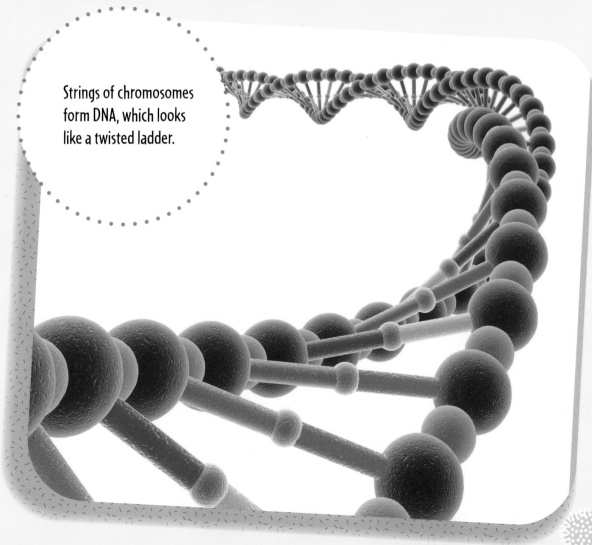

Strings of chromosomes form DNA, which looks like a twisted ladder.

Meiosis and mitosis

There are two types of cell division, called **meiosis** and **mitosis**. During meiosis, a parent cell divides twice to produce four daughter cells. These four cells are called germ cells. The germ cells in men are sperm, and in women they are eggs.

Human parent cells have 46 chromosomes, but germ cells have 23 chromosomes. Eggs come from a mother and carry half her genes. Sperm come from a father and carry half his genes. When a human egg and sperm unite, the **embryo** (unborn or unhatched offspring) that results will have a complete set of 46 chromosomes.

Once an embryo is formed, it needs to grow into a living animal. This is when mitosis takes over. The cells in the embryo do not get larger. They duplicate over and over again, making exact copies. Organs, bones, and tissue form as each type of cell divides into millions of new cells.

This cell is dividing into two equal cells, each with the same **organelles**.

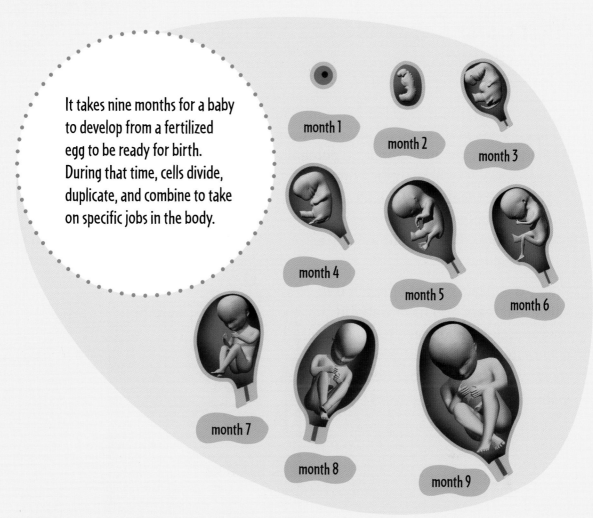

It takes nine months for a baby to develop from a fertilized egg to be ready for birth. During that time, cells divide, duplicate, and combine to take on specific jobs in the body.

month 1

month 2

month 3

month 4

month 5

month 6

month 7

month 8

month 9

What are stem cells?

In humans and most other animals, bodies produce a type of cell called a stem cell. These cells duplicate through mitosis. They can also **differentiate** and develop into different types of cells.

Cells begin to duplicate when they sense that there is plenty of food to support new cells. For **protists**, when food is available, the single cell splits in two and forms a new protist. For mammals, such as humans and whales, the embryo feeds and grows inside the mother. For birds, reptiles, and amphibians that lay eggs, the food an embryo needs is in the yolk and white of the egg.

Mitosis continues throughout an animal's life, whether the animal is growing or not. Your body is a cell factory. You need to make new cells to replace old or dead cells. The way your body makes these new, replacement cells is through mitosis.

Why Do Cells Need Water?

Without water, there is no life. Most animal bodies are made up of 40 to 80 percent water. Humans are made up of about 60 percent water on average throughout a lifetime. That does not mean fresh water, like we drink. Our bodies mix water and minerals to make water that is about as salty as Earth's oceans.

Water is a major part of blood. It is in **saliva** and tears. You have water in your muscles and organs. Your body uses water to help digest food, and to carry waste out of your body in **urine** (liquid waste) and **feces**.

Human cells—like all animal cells—need water to survive.

How much water is enough?

Humans should drink eight 8-ounce glasses of water a day. The reason is that your body constantly loses water from sweating, breathing, and passing waste. Water supports your cells. Without water, cells shrivel and die. Waste chemicals in the body cannot be passed in urine, and they become like poison. The body poisons itself. As lack of water progresses, organs stop working, and a person would die.

Too much water is not good, either. With too much water, cells bloat (swell) and the cell **membranes** explode. Cells need a chemical balance to work properly. With too much water flowing through your body, minerals and vitamins are washed out in urine before the body gets to use them fully.

Other animals and water

Not all animals need the same amount of water in their body. Elephants are big drinkers, gulping down more than 189 liters (50 gallons) of water a day. Camels do not need to drink every day. They store water in their **fat**. Kangaroo rats, however, never drink water. They get the water they need from the food they eat.

Despite what you read in children's stories, camels' humps do not store water. The water is stored in body fluids and fats.

How Do Cells Get Rid of Waste?

Cells like a tidy environment. As they work, cells create garbage. Some of the garbage is leftover chemicals. Some waste comes from broken parts, such as damaged **protein molecules**. Cells work constantly to get rid of waste.

The cell parts that break most often are proteins. A special kind of protein, called ubiquitin, goes around collecting broken strands of protein. Ubiquitin marks damaged protein for trash pickup.

A **lysosome** finds a marked bit of protein and surrounds it. Lysosomes transfer the waste into **vacuoles** for later trash removal. The lysosome binds to the vacuole containing waste, creating a new membrane-bound sac. When it is full, it moves to the cell **membrane**. The sac pushes open a small hole and pumps the waste out of the cell.

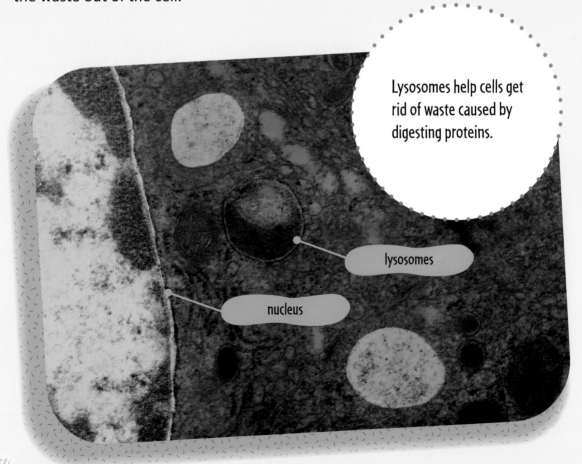

Lysosomes help cells get rid of waste caused by digesting proteins.

lysosomes

nucleus

When people sweat, glands in their skin push out water, salt, vitamin C, and chemical waste.

What kinds of waste?

One major waste product that cells handle is carbon dioxide. We breathe in air, use the oxygen, and exhale carbon dioxide. When you breathe in, lung cells take in oxygen. They transfer the oxygen to **red blood cells**. Blood cells deliver oxygen where is it needed and pick up the carbon dioxide waste, which is carried back to the lungs and thrown away as we exhale. The process of removing waste gas through breathing is called respiration, and it happens about 20,000 times a day in a human.

Our bodies work to get rid of chemical waste products that cells discard. Sweat and **urine** get rid of liquid waste and proteins. **Feces** carry waste salts, dead blood cells, dead **bacteria**, and other cell waste. If your body no longer needs a substance, cells will find a way to get rid of it.

Glossary

alga (plural: algae) plantlike organism that lives in water

amino acid carbon molecule that forms proteins

amoeba shapeless, one-celled animal

atom smallest unit of an element

bacterium (plural: bacteria) one-celled organism involved in digestion, decay, disease, and nitrogen in soil

carbohydrate sugar or starch

chemical compound substance made up of two or more elements

chromosome threadlike structure made of proteins that carry genes

compound microscope tool used to magnify items that are invisible to the naked eye

crustacean water-dwelling animals that have an outside skeleton

cytoplasm jellylike substance in cells

deoxyribonucleic acid (DNA) nucleic acids that carry the traits and characteristics of a living thing

differentiate to notice a difference

element substance that cannot be broken down into smaller substances

embryo unborn or unhatched offspring of an animal

endoplasmic reticulum (ER) network of tube-shaped membranes in cells

enzyme substance that increases the rate of chemical reactions in the body

euglena protist that acts like a plant or an animal

fat greasy or waxy substance produced by cells

feces solid animal waste

fission process of splitting a cell into two or more parts

gene basic unit that carries characteristics or physical traits of plants or animals

Golgi body complex part of a cell that gives off enzymes

hormone chemical substance that controls how cells react

infection effect of bacteria, a virus, or other invading substances on an animal body

insulate to cover or protect a substance, such as from heat or cold

lysosome organelle that digests food and proteins in a cell

meiosis type of cell division of eggs or sperm

membrane skin or protective layer

micron unit of length equal to one-millionth of a meter

mitochondrion (plural: mitochondria) organelle that deals with producing energy

mitosis type of cell division that produces two identical cells

molecule group of atoms bonded together into the smallest unit of a substance

neuron nerve cell

nucleic acid nucleotides that provide directions for cells

nucleus control center of a cell

nutrient substance in food that helps growth and health

organelle organized, functioning structure in an eukaryotic cell

paramecium (plural: paramecia) one-celled animal

platelet blood part that helps clotting

protein molecule that forms muscle and other essential body tissues

protist one-celled plant or animal

protozoa group of one-celled organisms in the kingdom Protista

red blood cell cell in animal blood that carries oxygen through the body

reproduce make a copy

ribonucleic acid (RNA) nucleic acid in cells that chooses genes and sends messages to cells about what they should do

ribosome particle containing RNA and proteins in cells

saliva watery liquid in the mouth containing enzymes that digest food

species group of living beings of the same type

urine liquid animal waste

vacuole space or pocket found in the cytoplasm of a cell

white blood cell a clear cell in blood that fights infections

Find Out More

Books to read

Johnson, Lori. *Cell Function and Specialization*. Chicago: Raintree, 2009.

Johnson, Rebecca L. *Mighty Animal Cells*. Minneapolis: Millbrook, 2008.

Latham, Donna. *Cells, Tissues, and Organs*. Chicago: Raintree, 2009.

Lee, Kimberly Fekany. *Cells*. Mankato, Minn.: Compass Point, 2008.

Light, Douglas B. *Cells, Tissues, and Skin*. New York: Chelsea House, 2009.

Mullins, Matt. *Super Cool Science Experiments: Cells*. Ann Arbor, Mich.: Cherry Lake, 2010.

Stille, Darlene R. A*nimal Cells: Smallest Units of Life*. Mankato, Minn.: Compass Point, 2006.

Websites

"Biology for Kids: Cell Structure"
www.biology4kids.com/files/cell_main.html
Learn more about cells and cell functions.

"BrainPOP: Cells"
www.brainpop.com/health/cellsandbodybasics/cells/preview.weml
BrainPOP offers an interactive, lively website with information about cells and how they are made.

"Cells Alive!"
www.cellsalive.com
See what happens to cells when viruses or bacteria attack.

"Inside a Cell"
http://learn.genetics.utah.edu/content/begin/cells/insideacell
The University of Utah gives you an opportunity to go inside a cell at this interactive website.

"Glow with the Flow"
http://explorations.ucsd.edu/biolum
Learn more about bioluminescence, including why and how animals glow in the dark.

"Your Gross and Cool Body: Human Skin"
http://yucky.discovery.com/flash/body/pg000146.html
Here is a place where you can discover the most interesting, weird, and fascinating information about skin cells and their jobs.

Become an expert

- Make a model of an animal cell using modeling clay. Add labels for all the parts.

- Create a chart about protozoa. Record the habitats (kind of place) where each species lives, what they eat, and how long they live. Draw an illustration of each protozoa species.

- Make a chart of vitamins and investigate how cells use each type of vitamin.

- Write a short story about cells. Imagine that you are a blood cell and describe your travels through the body in your story.

Index